LACROSSE

SCORE WITH STEM!

By Ellen Labrecque

Consultant: Tammy Englund, science educator

BEARPORT
PUBLISHING

Minneapolis, Minnesota

Credits

Cover and Title Page, © Benjamin Haslam/Dreamstime; 5, © Charles Fox/Philadelphia Inquirer/TNS/Newscom; 6, © Schaafb32/Shutterstock; 7, © bearden/iStock; 8, © bearden/iStock; 9, © Jason Mowry/Icon Sportswire/Newscom; 10–11, © WoodysPhotos/Shutterstock; 11, © Andy Mead/Icon Sportwire/Newscom; 12, © Sports Images/Dreamstime; 13, © Courtesy Catapult Sports; 14, © MileA/iStock; 15 top, courtesy Victorem Gear; 14–15 bottom, Jon Endow/Image of Sport/Newscom; 16, Courtesy Guardian Sports: PEARL LT lacrosse ball– SEI Certified, NOCSAE approved; 16–17, © Douglas Stringer/Icon Sportswire/Newscom; 18, © DAC Photos/iStock; 19 top © Sports Images/Dreamstime; 19 bottom, Wikimedia; 20, © Aaron M. Sprecher/AP Images; 21, © Aspenphoto/Dreamstime; 22 left, © bpalmer/iStock; 22 right, © Vincent Giordano Photo/Shutterstock; 23, © Robin Alam/Icon Sportswire/Newscom; 24–25, Courtesy Loyola University; 27, © Douglas Stringer/Icon Sportswire/Newscom; 29 © bpalmer/iStock

Bearport Publishing Company
Minneapolis, Minnesota
President: Jen Jenson
Director of Product Development: Spencer Brinker
Senior Editor: Allison Juda
Associate Editor: Charly Haley
Designer: Colin O'Dea

Produced by Shoreline Publishing Group LLC
Santa Barbara, California
Designer: Patty Kelley
Editorial Director: James Buckley Jr.

Library of Congress Cataloging-in-Publication Data

Names: Labrecque, Ellen, author.
Title: Lacrosse : score with STEM! / By Ellen Labrecque.
Description: Minneapolis, Minnesota : Bearport Publishing Company, [2022] |
   Series: Sports STEM | Includes bibliographical references and index.
Identifiers: LCCN 2021003687 (print) | LCCN 2021003688 (ebook) | ISBN
   9781636911793 (library binding) | ISBN 9781636911861 (paperback) | ISBN
   9781636911939 (ebook)
Subjects: LCSH: Lacrosse--Juvenile literature. | Science--Study and
   teaching--Juvenile literature. | Technology--Study and
   teaching--Juvenile literature.
Classification: LCC GV989.14 .L34 2022 (print) | LCC GV989.14 (ebook) |
   DDC 796.36/2--dc23
LC record available at https://lccn.loc.gov/2021003687
LC ebook record available at https://lccn.loc.gov/2021003688

For more information, write to Bearport Publishing, 5357 Penn Avenue South, Minneapolis, MN 55419. Printed in the United States of America.

Contents

Lacrosse and STEM

With just a few seconds left in the lacrosse game, the score is tied. The attacker cradles the ball close to the goal. She sees an opening in the defense. With both hands gripping her stick, she shoots the ball hard. It zips through the air! The ball flies past the goalie into the top corner of the net. Score! The attacker scored because of her strong shot—but she had some help from STEM, too!

SCIENCE: From shooting on goal to facing off against an opponent, the game of lacrosse plays out according to the rules of physics.

TECHNOLOGY: Discover how wearable tech and **radar guns** tell us more about the game.

ENGINEERING: The latest lacrosse stick, ball, and field designs help teams play better than ever.

MATH: Information about teams and players is gathered as numbers called **stats**. A winning score is just the beginning!

After a goal, it's time for a celebration!

Holding onto the Ball

The midfielder sprints down the field with the ball in her stick's pocket. She cradles the ball in the pocket by twisting the stick back and forth in her hands. Even as she runs through the defense, the ball does not fly out. How does it stay put?

Cradling also keeps the ball in the perfect position to fire an accurate shot.

The Perfect Twist

As a player runs with a lacrosse ball, a **force** called **inertia** causes the ball to move in a straight line. Cradling keeps the ball in the netted pocket. When the player twists the stick, the stick's motion around the ball holds the ball in the pocket.

Contact between players is allowed in men's lacrosse, so defenders can slam into opponents with body **checks**. For this reason, men's lacrosse sticks have deeper pockets to help them hold onto the ball. Women's lacrosse sticks have shallower pockets, which helps players make quick passes.

Need for Speed

The attacker races toward his opponent's goal. He flies past a defender. As he drives in, he rips a fast shot toward the bottom of the goal. Score!

In shots like these, the ball can reach speeds of more than 100 miles per hour (160.9 kph)! How do attackers use physics to make such powerful shots?

Work Together

The ball's speed comes from using the stick as a **lever**. A player puts one hand near the bottom of the stick and the other hand near the middle. The bottom hand pulls the stick back and the top hand pushes the stick forward. The bottom hand helps aim the ball, and the top hand generates the force that creates speed.

A moving player plants his front foot right before shooting the ball. This allows him to convert his running **momentum** into shooting power. The harder a player plants his foot, the faster his shot will go.

The Face-Off

Two men's lacrosse players crouch down across from each other. They're holding their sticks on the ground, inches apart. The referee places the ball on the ground. When the ref blows the whistle, the two players use their stick heads to press down on the ball. But only one of the players will win this face-off and get control!

Players in a face-off also use the force of pushing against each other to try to get an advantage.

Powerful Stuff

Face-offs are won by a force called **torque**. Torque is created when a player rotates the stick head to clamp down on the ball. The player who can rotate his stick faster and with more force will get the ball first and usually wins the face-off. Strength, speed, and physics all work together.

Face-offs in women's lacrosse are called draws. In a draw, the ball is held in the air between the netting of two players' sticks. Then, the players move their arms and elbows to create **leverage**. This helps them push the ball up and out in the direction they want it to go.

Wearable Tech

The game is tied in the fourth period. But the team's star player is exhausted. He's moving slower because he's tired. Suddenly, one of his opponents zooms by to score the winning goal! What can help the tired player prepare for the next game?

Tracking Energy

Many lacrosse players wear **GPS** monitors while they train. These **sensors** track where and how fast a player moves on the field. Using this **data**, coaches can help players plan their training so they will have plenty of energy on game day.

Sensors go into a pocket under the shirt.

GPS technology can tell a coach if a player is running too much in warm-up before the game even starts! They may use this data to cut down on pregame running so the player is able to run for longer during the game.

High-Speed Shooting

Lacrosse star Paul Rabil is one of the fastest shooters in the game. His shots have reached 111 miles per hour (178.6 kph)! It takes a lot of practice to get a lacrosse ball to move that fast. But how do we know how fast Rabil's shot is going?

Radar Readings

A lacrosse team can use a radar gun to measure the speed of players' shots. This device sends out radio waves. Once the waves hit a moving ball, they bounce back to a sensor in the device. By measuring how quickly the waves returned, a radar gun can calculate the speed of the ball. The result is displayed on the radar gun's screen.

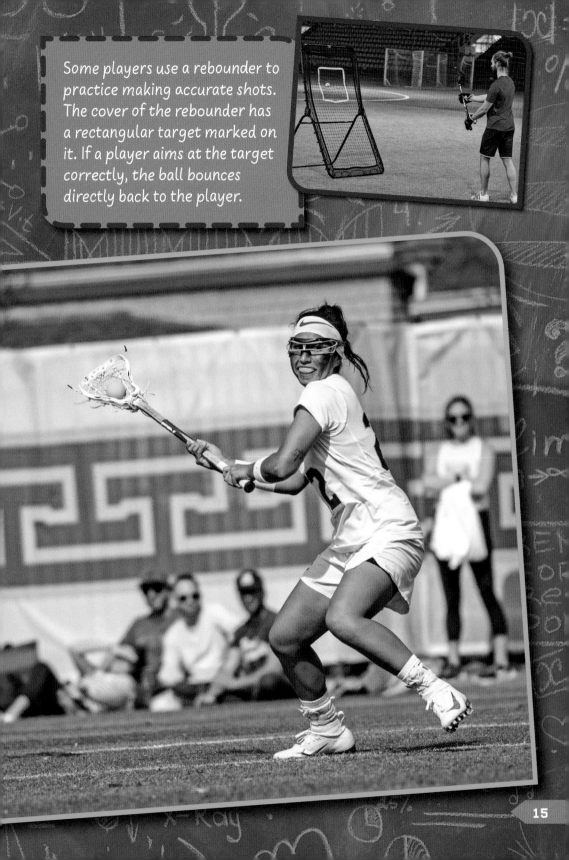

Some players use a rebounder to practice making accurate shots. The cover of the rebounder has a rectangular target marked on it. If a player aims at the target correctly, the ball bounces directly back to the player.

Follow the Bouncing Ball

Lacrosse balls are the hardest and bounciest kind of sports balls. Players use this to their advantage by mastering the bounce shot. When a lacrosse ball hits the ground and bounces back up, it spins differently than it does in a direct shot. This spinning makes the bounce shot hard for a goalie to stop.

Rubber and Texture

Lacrosse balls are made of a type of rubber that is especially hard and **elastic**—ideal for bounce shots. The balls also have a slight texture on the surface. This texture makes the balls easier to grip, cradle, and shoot in any weather condition. It also helps with spin and accuracy during bounces and passes.

A player bounces the ball past the goalie!

Players often practice with balls that are less bouncy than game balls. This helps develop skills without having to chase after missed shots! There is also less chance of injury when using practice balls inside because they are less likely to cause harm bouncing back from walls and the floor.

Stick It to Them

The first lacrosse sticks were made from wood, but they were heavy and difficult to use. Soon, engineers created new sticks using **carbon fiber** and plastic. These sticks are both lightweight and very tough. Carbon fiber sticks don't break as easily as wooden ones.

What a Mesh!

Engineers also worked to create a different kind of mesh netting in the stick's pocket. This netting was traditionally made from leather and would get stretched out of shape after a lot of use. The newer style of mesh is made from rope or nylon coated with wax, which keeps its shape better. With sturdy pockets, players can make more accurate passes and shots.

These wood sticks have mesh made from leather.

Lacrosse sticks can come in many different colors.

A goalie uses a stick with a much larger pocket than other players' sticks. The larger pocket helps the goalie catch shots speeding toward the goal.

The Playing Field

It's the middle of a close game, and players from both teams are giving their all. The players move easily and skillfully across the artificial turf field. Turf made years ago was much more difficult to play on because it was hard and slippery. What makes this new artificial turf so much better?

The Secret Is Infill

Today, lacrosse is played on both natural grass and artificial turf. The turf uses human-made fibers that look and feel like grass but that last a long time. Engineers create new turfs to be softer and bouncier, too. They do this by filling in the space around the fibers with infill—tiny pieces of crushed material. Infill might include cork, shells, walnuts, or pieces of clean rubber. Fields with turfs that have infill are safer for players if they fall.

Rubber pellets in infill bounce up after a player steps on them.

Engineers design turf that allows players to move easily.

Stick vs. Stick

As the midfielder sprints down the field, she looks ahead and sees her teammate open for a pass. She pulls the bottom of her stick back to release the ball. The ball flies through the air toward her teammate. Suddenly, a defender's long stick rises, snatching the ball before it reaches its target. Interception!

Long and Short

Defenders usually play with longer sticks than attacking players do. Math helps explain why this is an advantage. A longer stick can reach a greater **area** for the defender to protect. But for the attackers, smaller sticks help make quicker shots.

Offensive sticks are usually 40 to 42 inches (101 to 106 cm)

Defensive sticks are usually 52 to 72 in (132 to 183 cm)

It's stick vs. stick. Defenders can use their longer sticks to block attacking players.

Tracking Top Scorers

Top scorers in lacrosse will fire shot after shot at the goalie, trying to get the ball into the net. One way of determining the best shooters is by counting the goals they score. But what about accuracy? Whose shots go in the net most often?

High Percentage Wins

A lacrosse player is **ranked** by their shooting percentage. This compares the number of goals a player scores with the number of shots they take in order to show how accurate the player's shots are. To find this stat, divide the number of goals by the number of shots taken, and then move the decimal point two places to the right. In 2019, Sam Fiedler of Loyola University had the best shooting percentage in Division I women's college lacrosse. She scored 53 goals out of 79 shots. That gave her a 67.1 shooting percentage.

Sam Fiedler's high shooting percentage made her a star.

The Right Position

The goalie watches the ball as members of the opposing team pass it from one player to the next. As the ball moves, the goalie adjusts his position in front of the goal. He wants to be in the best spot to stop the ball. The goalie always tries to cover the most area to block an opponent's shooting **angle**.

The Goalie Arc

Goalies always want to be between the shooter and the goal. They move to one of five different positions, depending on where the shooter is. This makes the shooting angle smaller and gives the shooter less area to aim at. Together, the five positions are called the goalie **arc**.

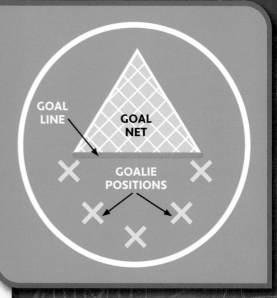

The X's show the goalie arc—the positions a goalie takes as shooters move around the goal.

The goalie has moved to the best position to block the most angles from the shooter.

Do the Math!

Ready to do some lacrosse math? Learn how to calculate three types of stats. Then, do the math to find out which players had the best stats.

Points Total

The best offensive players are recognized for their total number of points, which combines their goals scored and their assists. Add the assists and goals for each player below to find out who has the most points.

1. Which player has the higher points total?

PLAYER	ASSISTS	GOALS
Kenzie Kent	75	52
Sam Apuzzo	30	94

Shooting Percentage

A percentage is a part of a whole number expressed in hundredths. To find the shooting percentage, divide the number of times a player scored goals by the number of shots taken. Then move the decimal point two places to the right.

2. Which player has the higher shooting percentage?

PLAYER	GOALS	SHOTS
Chris Young	44	74
Clarke Petterson	44	79

Per-Game Averages

A per-game average is a number that helps compare skill levels for players who have played in different numbers of games. To find it, divide each player's stat by the number of games played.

3. Saves are key to being a good goalie. Which player had the higher saves-per-game average?

PLAYER	SAVES	GAMES PLAYED
Jacob Stover	250	17
Owen McElroy	171	16

4. You can't score if you don't shoot! Which of these players had the highest average number of shots taken per game?

PLAYER	SHOTS	GAMES PLAYED
Erin Cohen	127	16
Tamika Carter	141	21

Answers:
1. Kent had 127 points, 3 more than Apuzzo's 124 points.
2. Young's shot percentage was 59.5 percent, a little higher than Petterson's 55.7 percent.
3. Stover made 14.7 saves per game, which was more than McElroy's 10.7.
4. Carter took more shots in total, but her 6.71 shots-per-game average was lower than Cohen's 7.93 average.

Glossary

angle the space between two lines that meet at a common endpoint

arc a path that follows a curve

area the size of a certain space

carbon fiber a lightweight material used to strengthen other materials

checks hits to the body of a player or a player's stick, intended to knock the ball loose from the stick

data information often in the form of numbers

elastic able to stretch easily

force the push or pull of an object

GPS Global Positioning System; used to show location and movement on Earth

inertia the force that keeps an object at rest or moving

lever a long bar that rests on a support and is used to move an object

leverage the action of using a lever to move something from one point to another point

momentum strength or force of something gained while in motion

radar guns handheld devices that measure the speed of a moving object

ranked placed in order from best to worst

sensors electronic devices that record or gather and send information

stats short for statistics; information stated as numbers

torque a force that rotates or twists something

Read More

Marquardt, Meg. *Women in Lacrosse (She's Got Game).* Lake Elmo, MN: Focus Readers, 2020.

Wells, Don. *Lacrosse (For the Love of Sports).* New York: AV2 by Weigl, 2020.

Wiener, Gary. *Lacrosse: Science on the Field (Science Behind Sports).* New York: Lucent Press, 2018.

Learn More Online

1. Go to **www.factsurfer.com**

2. Enter "**STEM Lacrosse**" into the search box.

3. Click on the cover of this book to see a list of websites.

Index

About the Author

Ellen Labrecque is a former editor at *Sports Illustrated Kids*. She has written over 100 books for children. She played lacrosse and basketball in college and loves to run. She lives in Bucks County, Pennsylvania, with her husband and two kids.